A HOLISTIC GUIDE TO STRESS-FREE LIVING

STEPHANIE DIAMOND

Table of Contents

Introduction

Are you feeling overwhelmed, stressed, or just plain frazzled? If so, you're not alone. In today's fast-paced world, it's easy to get caught up in the hustle and bustle and forget to take time for ourselves. But here's the thing: relaxation isn't just a luxury, it's a necessity. Studies show that relaxation can have profound benefits for your physical and mental health, from reducing stress and improving sleep to boosting your mood and increasing your productivity.

Chapter 1

THE PURSUIT OF PEACE: WHY RELAXATION MATTERS

Stress! It's the silent assassin that lurks in the shadows, sapping your energy and stealing your joy. But fear not, intrepid reader! This chapter will arm you with the knowledge and tools you need to take on stress like a relaxation warrior. Get ready to say goodbye to that tight chest, clenched jaw, and racing heart. We're gonna unleash the relaxation beast within and send stress running for the hills!"

- Stress can cause all kinds of nasty things like high blood pressure, insomnia, and even heart disease.

- Relaxation can reduce stress hormones and increase feel-good hormones, resulting in a calmer, happier you.

-Relaxation techniques like deep breathing, progressive muscle relaxation, and guided imagery can be practiced anywhere, anytime, with no equipment or expensive gym membership required.

- Taking the time to relax is an investment in your health, happiness, and overall quality of life.

The science of the relaxation response

- The relaxation response is a physiological state characterized by a decrease in heart rate, blood pressure, and muscle tension, and an increase in brain wave frequency.

- It's essentially the opposite of the fight-or-flight response.

- The relaxation response is associated with the parasympathetic nervous system, which promotes rest and recovery.

- Studies show that the relaxation response can improve immune function, decrease inflammation, and reduce anxiety and depression.

- Deep breathing, meditation, and progressive muscle relaxation are all proven techniques to elicit the relaxation response.

Different relaxation techniques and how they work.

- Deep breathing: inhaling and exhaling slowly can stimulate the parasympathetic nervous system, which can lower heart rate and blood pressure.

- Meditation: focusing on a mantra or your breath can help quiet the mind, reduce stress, and increase mindfulness.

- Progressive muscle relaxation: tensing and relaxing different muscle groups can decrease muscle tension and promote relaxation.

- Yoga: various poses and breathing techniques in yoga can reduce stress and promote relaxation through increased flexibility and mindfulness.

- Guided imagery: visualizing relaxing scenes and images can decrease stress and promote relaxation through visualization.

The benefits of relaxation for physical and mental health
- Reduced blood pressure
- Decreased risk of heart disease
- Improved sleep quality
- Increased energy and productivity
- Reduced anxiety and depression
- Enhanced immunity
- Lower inflammation levels
- Improved cognitive function and memory
- Better emotional regulation and resilience

Basically, relaxation is like a panacea for all that ails ya.

How to make relaxation a daily habit

Buckle up, 'cause this is where things get practical! Here are some tips for making relaxation a habit:

- Schedule relaxation time in your day like any other appointment.

- Start small and build up gradually, like 5 minutes a day.

- Experiment with different techniques to find what works for you.

- Incorporate relaxation into your existing routine, like during your commute or before bed.

- Create a relaxing environment, like a comfy chair, dim lighting, and calming music.

- Make relaxation a priority and commit to it, like you would to brushing your teeth or eating healthy.

Overcoming common relaxation obstacles like time, motivation, and distractions

- Time: Prioritize relaxation by blocking out time in your calendar and being mindful of not over scheduling.

- Motivation: Remind yourself of the benefits and try to view relaxation as an investment in your well-being, not a luxury.

- Distractions: Create a distraction-free environment by turning off notifications, muting your phone, and avoiding multi-tasking during relaxation time.

- Mindset: Reframe your mindset and view relaxation as a necessity, not an indulgence.

Tips for creating a relaxing environment and cultivating a relaxation mindset.

- Surround yourself with calming colors, like blue or green.

- Use essential oils, like lavender or chamomile, to create a soothing scent.

- Reduce noise by using white noise machines or earplugs.

- Keep your space organized and clutter-free.

- Avoid screens and bright lights before bedtime to promote relaxation and better sleep.

- Practice mindfulness and gratitude to cultivate a relaxation mindset.

- Create a bedtime routine to signal to your brain and body that it's time to wind down.

Chapter 2

THE SCIENCE OF STRESS: UNDERSTANDING THE HORMONES AND NEUROTRANSMITTERS THAT DRIVE STRESS.

Stress is a ubiquitous part of modern life, and it's not just a state of mind - it's a complex physiological response with far-reaching consequences for our health and well-being. But what exactly is stress? And how does it work?

In this chapter, we'll take a deep dive into the biological underpinnings of stress and its effects on the body and mind. From hormones to neurotransmitters, we'll uncover the intricate mechanisms that drive stress response and explore how chronic stress can lead to physical and psychological problems.

- Stress hormones like cortisol and adrenaline are produced by the adrenal glands and play a key role in the body's fight-or-flight response.

- The hypothalamus in the brain regulates stress response by sending signals to the pituitary gland, which then signals the adrenal glands to release stress hormones.

- Neurotransmitters like norepinephrine and serotonin are involved in mood and stress response, and imbalances in these chemicals can contribute to anxiety and depression.

- The immune system's response to stress, including the effects of chronic stress on inflammation and disease susceptibility.

- The link between stress and cardiovascular disease, including high blood pressure and heart disease.

- The impact of stress on sleep, and the role of sleep in regulating stress and mood. The importance of a healthy lifestyle, including exercise and nutrition, in managing stress.

Chapter 3

MINDFULNESS AND MEDITATION: HARNESSING THE POWER OF PRESENCE.

In a world of constant stimulation and distraction, finding peace and stillness can feel like a lost art. But with the practices of mindfulness and meditation, you can tap into a reservoir of inner calm and cultivate a greater sense of presence in your daily life.

This chapter delves into the transformative power of mindfulness and meditation, exploring the scientific evidence for their benefits and offering practical tips for incorporating these practices into your routine.

Presence is all about being fully engaged in the moment, free from distractions and mental chatter.

Mindfulness and meditation can help you cultivate presence by teaching you to focus your attention and be more aware of your thoughts and emotions in real-time.

Presence can lead to increased creativity, problem-solving abilities, and overall mental clarity.

By cultivating presence, you can also enhance your relationships and increase your overall satisfaction with life.

Chapter 4

FINDING FLOW: RIDING THE WAVE OF FOCUS AND CREATIVITY.

Flow is that magical state of being where you're so engrossed in what you're doing, you lose track of time and everything else around you. It's a state of effortless focus and creativity that many artists, athletes, and high performers chase after. But guess what, with mindfulness and meditation, you can train your brain to access that flow state and tap into your full potential. In this chapter, we'll explore how to enter flow, the science behind it, and how to harness its power to unlock your best self.

The neuroscience behind flow, including the role of dopamine, endorphins, and other chemicals in the brain that contribute to the flow state.

- Dopamine is a neurotransmitter associated with motivation, pleasure, and reward. During flow, dopamine levels increase, leading to a sense of enjoyment and motivation to continue the activity.

- Endorphins are natural painkillers produced by the brain and released during flow. They create a sense of euphoria and well-being.

- Serotonin is another neurotransmitter involved in mood regulation and happiness. It's also elevated during flow, contributing to a sense of calm and contentment.

The impact of flow on learning and memory, and how it can enhance cognitive performance.

- Studies show that flow can enhance information processing and memory consolidation. During flow, the brain is more efficient at encoding and retrieving information.

- Flow can also improve attention and concentration, making it easier to focus on tasks and filter out distractions.

- It can also promote a state of "flow learning," where new skills and concepts are acquired more easily and are more likely to be retained.

- The combination of focus, creativity, and enhanced memory can lead to breakthroughs and innovative thinking.

- The link between flow and positive emotions, including happiness, joy, and a sense of fulfillment.

- Flow can lead to a sense of "autotelic" experience - an experience that is intrinsically rewarding and enjoyable in and of itself, without the need for external rewards.

- People in flow report feeling a sense of "being in the zone" - fully immersed in the present moment, free from self-consciousness, and at their best.

- Flow can also promote a sense of "self-actualization" - the feeling of reaching one's full potential and achieving personal goals and aspirations.

How to cultivate a mindset that supports flow, such as embracing challenges, setting challenging yet achievable goals, and embracing a growth mindset.

- Adopt a growth mindset - believe that abilities can be developed and that challenges are opportunities for growth.

- Set specific, challenging, and achievable goals that stretch you just beyond your current abilities.

- Embrace challenges and setbacks as learning opportunities rather than failures.

- Practice mindfulness and cultivate a sense of curiosity and openness.

- Surround yourself with a supportive and challenging environment, with mentors and peers who encourage you to push yourself and grow.

Chapter 5

THE POWER OF NATURE: CONNECTING WITH THE OUTDOORS FOR STRESS RELEASE

Have you ever stepped outside and felt instantly calmer, more connected, and less stressed? Turns out, there's a scientific explanation for that magic. Nature has some seriously underrated healing powers. In this chapter, we'll explore the incredible benefits of connecting with the great outdoors, from the physical perks like lowered blood pressure and increased energy, to the mental and emotional boosts like reduced anxiety and improved focus.

- One of the major benefits of spending time in nature is the boost in positive emotions, including awe, inspiration, and gratitude. These emotions can improve overall mental health and increase resilience to stress.

- Exposure to natural environments can also enhance creativity and problem-solving skills, which can help alleviate stress caused by work or personal challenges.

- Physical activity in nature, like hiking or gardening, can release endorphins, which are natural mood-boosters and stress-busters.

The importance of green spaces in urban environments, and how they can improve mental health in densely populated areas.
urban green spaces are the unsung heroes of mental health!
- Studies show that access to nature in cities can reduce symptoms of depression, anxiety, and stress.

- Green spaces provide a respite from the hustle and bustle of city life, and can help people feel calmer and more centered.

- Access to nature in cities can also reduce the effects of "urban heat islands," which are areas with higher temperatures due to heat-trapping buildings and paved surfaces, and can contribute to poor mental and physical health.

The role of sunlight and fresh air in regulating circadian rhythms and improving sleep, which in turn reduces stress and improves mood.

- Sunlight is essential for the production of melatonin, a hormone that regulates the sleep-wake cycle. Exposure to sunlight during the day can help the body establish a regular sleep pattern, which in turn reduces stress and improves mood.

- Fresh air and exercise during the day can help people sleep better at night, which is crucial for overall mental and physical health.

- Studies have linked poor sleep to higher levels of cortisol, the stress hormone, and a higher risk of depression and anxiety.

The impact of outdoor activities on social connections, which are crucial for emotional well-being and stress management.
Social connections are like the secret sauce of mental health.
- Outdoor activities like group sports, hiking, or even just hanging out in a park can provide opportunities for social interaction and community-building, which are crucial for emotional well-being and stress management.

- Social support has been shown to reduce stress and improve resilience to stressors, and outdoor activities provide a natural and low-pressure setting for building connections.

- Outdoor activities can also provide opportunities for connection with nature, which has been shown to have positive effects on mental health.

Chapter 6

CALMING THE CHAOS: MINDFUL TECHNIQUES FOR EVERYDAY STRESS.

In today's fast-paced world, stress is a constant companion. But what if we told you that you can reduce stress in a simple, effective way without even leaving your home? That's where mindful techniques come in. In this chapter, we'll explore a range of techniques that you can integrate into your daily routine to reduce stress and promote well-being. Get ready to unwind, relax, and cultivate a sense of inner peace.

Techniques are :
- Progressive muscle relaxation, where you systematically tense and relax different muscle groups to reduce tension and anxiety.
It involves tensing and releasing different muscle groups, starting with the feet and working up to the face.

- As you relax each muscle, you focus on the sensations of tension leaving the body and breathing deeply.

- This technique helps reduce the physical symptoms of stress and anxiety, like muscle tension, headaches, and shallow breathing.

- It also helps to redirect attention away from anxious thoughts and worries.

- Overall, progressive muscle relaxation can help to promote a sense of calm and relaxation throughout the body.

- Guided imagery, where you use your imagination to visualize peaceful scenes and reduce stress.

- Mindful listening, where you focus on actively listening to others without judgment to improve communication and reduce stress.

- Body scan meditation, where you focus on each part of your body to become more aware of physical sensations and release tension.

Mindful walking, where you focus on the sensations of your feet on the ground and your surroundings to reduce stress.

The ancient art of mindful walking. It's like a mini-vacation for your brain! Here are some of the ways mindful walking can reduce stress:

- It gets you out in nature, which has been shown to have calming effects.

- Walking increases blood flow to the brain, which can help reduce stress hormones like cortisol.

- Focusing on your surroundings and sensations can help take your mind off of stressful thoughts.

- Walking can also help improve overall fitness and reduce the risk of chronic diseases like heart disease and diabetes, which can be major stressors

Mindful breathing techniques, like diaphragmatic breathing and 4-7-8 breathing, to reduce stress and promote relaxation.
Sure thing! Here are some deets on those techniques:

Diaphragmatic breathing, also known as belly breathing, involves breathing deeply from the diaphragm rather than the chest, which can help slow down the heart rate and lower blood pressure.

The 4-7-8 breathing technique involves breathing in for 4 seconds, holding for 7 seconds, and breathing out for 8 seconds, which can help activate the parasympathetic nervous system (the "rest and digest" mode).

- Mindful acceptance, where you learn to accept and acknowledge negative emotions without judgment to reduce stress and improve well-being.

Mindful communication, where you practice active listening and empathetic communication to improve relationships and reduce stress.

Mindful communication involves using active listening techniques like:
- Paying full attention to the speaker, without interrupting or judging.

- Paraphrasing and reflecting back what the speaker said to show that you're paying attention.

- Asking open-ended questions to encourage deeper conversation.

- Using nonverbal cues like eye contact, nodding, and leaning in to show interest.

- Avoiding assumptions and jumping to conclusions, and being willing to clarify and confirm understanding.

Chapter 7

MUSIC THERAPY

Ready to crank up the tunes and turn down the stress? Music therapy is a powerful tool for reducing stress and promoting relaxation. Whether you're listening to soothing melodies, belting out a ballad, or strumming a guitar, music can have a profound effect on your mental and physical well-being. In this chapter, we'll dive into the science behind music therapy, explore different types of music that can help reduce stress, and provide tips for incorporating music into your stress-busting routine. So, plug in those headphones and get ready to jam your way to relaxation!"

Here are some key points about music therapy

- It can help to reduce symptoms of depression, anxiety, and stress, as well as improve mood and well-being.

- It's a non-invasive, drug-free approach that can be used in conjunction with other forms of therapy.

- Music therapy can be tailored to an individual's needs and preferences, making it a flexible and personalized form of therapy.

- It can be used in a variety of settings, including hospitals, schools, and private practice.

- Improve cognitive functioning, such as memory and attention span.

- Enhance social skills and communication abilities, especially for individuals with autism or other communication disorders.

- Support physical rehabilitation, such as in patients recovering from stroke or other neurological conditions.

- Aid in pain management, reducing the need for medication in some cases.
It's pretty amazing how much power music can have on the body and mind.

Chapter 8

MASSAGE THERAPY

Get ready to rub out the stress with our ultimate guide to massage therapy! We're covering all the benefits, from reducing muscle tension to boosting the immune system, and beyond. From Swedish massage to deep tissue work, we'll explore the different techniques and their effects on the body and mind. It's time to treat yourself to some relaxation and healing, one massage at a time!

The magic of massage therapy:

- It can reduce headaches and migraines by relaxing the muscles in the head and neck.

- Massage can help improve joint mobility and range of motion in patients with arthritis and other conditions that cause joint stiffness.

- It's an effective way to reduce anxiety and promote relaxation, as it triggers the release of endorphins, the body's natural painkillers.

- Massage can help alleviate the symptoms of fibromyalgia and chronic fatigue syndrome, which often include pain, fatigue, and depression.

- Massage therapy can improve athletic performance by reducing muscle soreness and increasing flexibility.

- It can be a helpful treatment for people with depression, as it has been shown to improve mood and reduce symptoms of depression.

- Massage therapy can also improve skin health by increasing circulation and promoting the elimination of toxins from the body.

- it can be used to alleviate symptoms of insomnia, by relaxing the body and promoting restful sleep.